DEVIANTS

DEVIANTS

PETER KLINE

STEPHEN F. AUSTIN STATE UNIVERSITY PRESS
NACOGDOCHES TEXAS

Stephen F. Austin State University Press
P.O. Box 13007, SFA Station
Nacogdoches, TX   75962-3007
sfasu.edu/sfapress
sfapress@sfasu.edu

Book Design: Laura Davis

Manufactured in the United States of America

LIBRARY OF CONGRESS IN PUBLICATION DATA
Kline, Peter
Deviants / Peter Kline

p. cm.
ISBN: 978-1-62288-029-4

1. Poetry. 2. American Poetry 3. Peter Kline

Distributed by Texas A&M Consortium
www.tamupress.com

CONTENTS

For my teachers

I

A passion most unsuiting such a man

—William Shakespeare, *Othello*

SWISH

I want to dress you as a man,
shark you in a fitted suit, iron-lined,
starched to your high white collar,
throatlocked in a double Windsor.
I want to draw you straight up and down
with the tight swish of silk slacks
around black captain's boots,
flatten you out with a greatcoat,
stack your shoulders up with pads.
I found a mashed porkpie hat
for you to tuck your hair up under
with a low brim for your lashes,
a watch like a gold-bar handshake.
A pair of lucky drawers
and you're him to the skin. I'll tie you in
with a thick strap of stitched leather.
You're my sexy, beautiful lover—
let's see if you can be my man.

First Fig

The openness is all. Yes
we say and the rest
follows. ——to the hollow
feeling of early morning
rueful memory fills in, listening
royally to the whistling kettle
overboiling. ——to the last call
pratfall, the catwalk climb
and skinny dip shimmy,
the bad-news nightcap.
Have you tried this?
daddy asks in the hot
in the back we say why
not, we say we'll pay
and are sadly happy.
We know. We
do it anyway.

MINOTAUR

You wound a ball of twine around my eyes
then pinned the end between my fingers.

You gowned me in white tissue
like a hothouse nectarine.

The furtive door at last unbarred, I was
amazed at the garden's suggestion

throating from vining flower-walls
in breaths that quickened with mine.

How long I lingered beneath
sun awnings and a stone-and-mortar sky,

only you know. For when I found the throneroom
festooned with pelvis bones,

the twin-fingered god on whose nether lip I hung
a kiss, a crape-gartered barb,

was you—you the pursued, yours
the bull's head draped with fragrant lash-black hair.

Axioms for The Anxiety

God alone knows what the world's supposed to be.
Looks at my cock: *What's that supposed to be?*

Somewhere between your back seat and this poem
there's a money shot where we're supposed to be.

Let's suppose I'm your husband, you my wife.
Who's your lover supposed to be?

I expressed my surprise. I wheedled and quibbled. At last, she said,
If it ain't on the menu, it ain't supposed to be.

A man for a woman for a woman for a man for a man.
Tell me again how it's supposed to be.

An Encounter

—There's something not-quite-right about you, he said.

—There's something not-quite-right about the way
you stand beside me, close enough to touch me.

I'm handsome. I know how to be gentle.

When I saw you crossing this way
I watched you cross over

straight to the spot, and stand beside me.

Foreplay to a handwashing—
the way you play with your drink,

smoothing droplets into the palm of your hand with your thumb;

with your thumb you smooth down hairs on the back of your hand.
If you know the song that's playing, you don't show it.

I'm careful. I know how to be lonely.

When I saw you cross over that way
I couldn't see you, couldn't stand the sight of you.

There's something—something not-quite-right

in the thing you're almost about to tell me,
what only a stranger makes safe.

You stand beside me, close enough

to tell me what no one else can hear;
I'll bend to you halfway.

Slow Jam

We spin around until we're spun
and test our grip with every twist.
It's risky dancing with a man.

Another scotch? Another gin?
I match my thirst against his thirst:
he spins around until we're spun.

The people good at saying *When*
are all tucked in. We do slow fast.
It's risky dancing with a man

you barely know. He isn't mine
but there's his chest against my chest.
We spin around until I'm spun.

Stranger, wrap me up again
while I convince myself to trust.
It's risky dancing with a man.

What am I—to have gone unseen
by those who saw me as I passed?
I spin and spin until I'm spun.
It's risky dancing with a man.

Poppyseed Aubade

I wake up late morning guilty from a guilty dream.
You're throat-deep in a sun-slough. Lie thou there.
How many years I've lived some stranger's life:
Mixing muffins—with such a deviant joy!

Second Fig

It's easy picking
out my kind—
straight in front
but bent behind

so we don't quite fit
in standard slots:
funny money.
Connect the dots:

We turn a sideways
question mark.
We elocute.
We cuss. We bark.

We beg for treats
then toss out bones.
Part skin-on-skin,
part silicone,

we make the bread
then fake the meat.
We're almost good
enough to eat.

CONSENT

After long nothing,
or days of asking
her, sometimes she
asks him. Usually
he's asleep already
and needs turning over,
opening. It's not easy
to find a way in
or even rouse him,
he's that faithful
to the dreaming. Needing
countertouch, overtingling,
knowing what's owed
she wriggles to the middle
or straddles his shoulders
backwards. Technically
consent means he
wakes and likes it.

Overture

It's happening again,
your old romance with death.
To be alone; alone.
Pink lips on a snaggletooth.

That old romance with death—
more strictly, a transaction.
Pink lips on a snaggletooth
or a pilsner glass of bourbon.

Forgive us our transactions?
Gotta pay your tab in full.
A pilsner glass of bourbon
for a nickel's worth of soul.

Gotta pay your tab in full.
Keep your hands flat on the table.
A nickel's worth of soul
buys a couple grand of trouble.

Keep your hands flat on the table.
Out to find yourself a piece,
in a couple grand of trouble,
you're getting dangerous.

Out to find yourself a place
to be alone, alone,
you're getting dangerous.
It's happening again.

DEVIANTS

> *Ich allein*
> *lebe und leide und lärme.*
> I alone
> live and suffer and howl.
> —Rainer Maria Rilke, *The Blindman's Song,*
> trans. Stephen Mitchell

1

Having been a lurker in dark corridors'
                                    half-open doors,
a malingerer in booths, a swiveler of stools,
a cocksure cruiser of bad-liver bars in borrowed clothes,

I go where everyone goes
and I go unseen.
                Here—take my hand and shake it.
Only I know where this hand has been.

2

I could have asked for it straight out, and got it.
I took the crooked way.
Now I see it sidelong,
                                    and pay for it on credit.

Till the pander-man knock-knocks
I prick my ears for come-and-get-it.
Don't let him cash me in
                                    till I collect.

3

I was worried, so I watched.
Watching was a thing to do
                              to bring me a little bit closer to you
whether or not you knew it.

(Oops! You missed a spot.)
                              Where you're rough I feel rough.
Looking's not enough. I want touch
that separates who's touching from who's touched.

4

I understand the way the killer works,
                            on three-week clocks.
A little itch, a little urge, a little ticklish hypothetical
then I splurge. And hustle to mop up.

To me it's not just stroke. More
than sore knees from keyhole-peeping
                            the pussy floss its teeth.
It never happened if I don't get caught.

.

5

To keep me in I had to keep it out.
And I needed to be kept:

     a risky secret,
I had more power the more I went unsaid.

Then I put it to my lips. I was pronounced
emphatically. My syllables were set.
Now I'm a byword, passed

     mouth to mouth to mouth.

6

While others get turned back, I pass,
but, passing, I grow less,
a blond john doe with a flinch and a wasted face.

I want new ways to be erased—
a righter lie, a stranger's cut-or-kiss.
Someday I'll pass right through

to someone else.

Triolet for a Bad Obsession

After I'm got, I never want to get.
They hit the buzzer, then they lock me in
and top me with a come-on like a threat.
I never want to get unless I've got
no money for the getting, and no spot
to put my body while the doing's done.
I only want to get until I'm got.
They hit the buzzer, then they lock me in.

THE ARGUMENT

The engine ticks and cools.
The windows gauze with breath.
At last, around us both
a rueful silence swells.

We seem like lovers here.
Not quite. We share a thing
for itching and for scratching.
Say more and go too far.

It's not just our shit luck
this trifling costs so dearly.
Too many penny cherries
make any stomach sick.

You think I'm weakening;
I'm sure that it won't fit.
If both of us are right
then one of us is wrong.

Love-Busker

I've got an ugly, but I'll never tell,
how pretty your please.
I've got a screw
tight, and wheels for wheels,
and an *.

I've got a real good thing—going—
so pardon my by-
your-leave. A way of opening
Ah and putting me
under. Over and out.

I've got muscles in here, somewhere.
A tooth that won't grow in. Spit
whistle, thumper finger,
tin can clang I'm
your one man band.

A memory of lapses. A good cold.
A winterized grin.
My boutique hard-sell soft-core
will pink you in.
It's rolled-gold bold.

If you want love in a king-size bed
beware my disease.
Symptoms:
catchall goodwill
and a right knee jitter.

On Seeing Fiona with Her New Lover

1

In this performance, I'm the watcher.
I'm plainclothes and narcotics.
Mine is the silence
of the majority, not the partner.
At best a bit player, a bit played out.
I'm known as a responsible customer.

2

She's the co-star to my idea,
scapegoat and sex symbol.
The action happens offstage, under the table,
but I see his thigh, I know how to read the angle.
I see myself in him: I
must keep hidden.

3

Act III, in which the hero *(He must
be a god, that man)* succumbs
to the watcher's inner life, whereby
at last he is made real. His death is optional.
It could be done
anywhere—even in her snug white bed.

LONG DIVISION

I've been taught to expect divide.
Keep your hands on your own side.
Birth cut me from my mother
but it started earlier:
before I even had a heart
they put me in a place apart
without a light, without a light.
No wonder if my heart's not right.

I've got a feel for separateness.
We both decided it was best,
considering how quietly
you became you, I became me
until we didn't know each other,
to civilly unswear together
what we'd sworn, and meant, for good.
Life parted us before death could.

The universal law is Split—
I tried to make the most of it;
Gave all my work away for free
and found I'd sold my dignity;
Severed all relationships
and wound up straddling the hips
of loneliness, the gentlejohn
who spends the night with everyone.

II

...my own hands carried me there.

—Walt Whitman, *Song of Myself*

CAMERADO

You've just picked up *Theodicies for Loners.*
The lipsticked tell-all of a made-up man.
Rebuttal to the post-postmodern cool.
Alternate bull's-eyes for the wrecking ball.

You're holding a worrystone for a child's hand.
A keepsake lifted from the excavation.
The part of the plant that's richest in nutrition.
A STAR MAP to the mansions of the dead.

You've opened up Pandora's other box.
The velvet buckle and the buttonfly.
The secret exit, wired with alarms.
You, too, are implicated in my schemes.

Reckoning

I got my mother's maybelline—
    it only caused me trouble.
I honed my higher faculties
    until the edge turned brittle.
The world I tried to coach with kindness
    kept on blithe and brutal.
So what can a stand-up guy lay down
    for a good seat at the table?

~

The way they taught it, I'd succeed
    if I just put in the work.
Busyness is its own reward;
    the money's just a perk.
Life can be like a fine champagne—
    just clench your teeth on the cork.
So I punched the daylight in, and spent
    my free time in the dark.

~

If love is the one part of god
    that's plummeted to earth,
I'd like to make a meteor
    out of my death and birth,
name all that falls, and, falling with it,
    shine my own name forth.
God's love is sweet, and decorous,
    but how much is it worth?

INVITATION

The ice bin clacks;
candles runnel their bottle sconces.

Friends waft in blinking, smiling over
the props of conviviality,

lime gin and pussy willow.
Fog turns the city to figment.

Good-time synth on the box
persuasively soft,

and the high and shag and prink and all
in a wobbly disco-spin.

Olive oil and onion,
denim and skin.

Everyone is delicious.
Everyone is accounted for

but the absentee.
It's easy to see

him: he makes gaps
where the talk won't go,

troubling it
as it flows around him.

Some speak and a place is made. The rest
accommodate.

There he is on the fire escape—
laughing in another language.

Taboo

I did a thing I wasn't meant to do.
No one made me. It was my decision.
Just something everybody knew was true
seemed iffy. I wanted further information.
In a part of town I'd never been before
an old man dressed me down with sideways eyes.
I found the camphored stairwell, second floor.
If I went up innocent, I came down wise.
What am I now? I sleep in the same bed,
pursue my ordinary daydream day,
greet my neighbors as one who has the right.
My dreams are the dreams of any righteous head,
perhaps. But picturing what I can't say,
you put it in my mouth. That's impolite.

UNIVERSAL MOVERS

We move the same packed box from house to house,
off the ancestral farm, now overgrown
with glorious, inedible rhododendrons
into the rented basement of a mud-lot
seeded for next spring. We sweat through shirts
to lug it six flights up to a Brooklyn flophouse
with a view of the subway station, ship it freight
to Porto, Tripoli, Piraeus, through
the Bosporus, points east, where one of us
will wait all day at customs just to claim it.
Rumors put us in a Baku teashop,
wrangling with the owner over the right
to commandeer his brother's pleasure boat
for the perilous night passage. How to convince
this gentleman? Our cargo is our right.
We fill out all the proper forms, insure
the contents (whatsoever they may be)
against flood, terrorism, sabotage,
human error and the will of god.
We learn the local pleasantries, and buy
blindness from every overcurious eye.

Press it to your ear: only the rustle
of your own cheek against it. Pierce its side:
no fleck of velveteen, no globe of blood.
Too small for a printing press, or plough, or cello,
too heavy for a gun, or a lock of hair,
it makes us wonder. Still, we can't raise
the courage or nostalgia to relieve us
of its mystery, and carry it like thieves
more ruthless for their inability
to find a buyer. We will not survive it.

PROTAGONIST

That was not the man.
—Robert Browning, *How It Strikes a Contemporary*

Maybe it's early, and he's taking the switchblade shortcut through
        the park,
a headlit billow of black jacket, an onward angle;
Or maybe he's out on Geary, nicotine-giddy, loitering
in the passing regard of passers-by, giving back shine;

Dissolved by dusk into a strange neighborhood, he studies
mimed intimacies broadcast from bay windows,
ambiguous flesh. He measures these lives out to the second
        decimal
and carries them with him, sheaved in butcher paper.

But if, one evening, stepping out from an alley
like a backlot actor who's wandered into the wrong picture,
emerging, straggling, struggling into shape
like a long-suppressed idea, who should appear
but you, one acquainted with his private life.
Then you call him by name: I must answer. I'm always afraid.

KARSILAMA

The kanunist's fingers blur like a conjurer's,
silk innuendos burlapped by his singing.
I sing along. "We are brothers now," he says,
fisting his heart. I believe him, lulled asleep
by the argument of dice in a metal bowl.
A hand on my skull. We emerge from kerosene
into clapboard alleys of the Golden Horn
filling the darkness with their disappearing.
I can't seem to keep my footing. A man leads me
by either arm. When at last my brother speaks,
it shakes my heart like a coin in a tambourine.

DIURNAL

This is how it is: I wake up early,
finish what I began the night before
and didn't finish—a poem, a pot of tea.
The rowers echo up from the reservoir.
Perhaps I stand a moment at the door
forgetting why I pause. Perhaps I name
the feeder birds and tomcats, for my pleasure.
The living things return me to my dream.

This is how it is: among the grim
and useless goads and parables, I find
the veiny stomach and the lobed intestine
of an eaten creature, ant-swarmed on the sand,
beside a white skiff tucked in the undergrowth.
That sound? The tireless grinding of my teeth.

Manzanita

Little apple. Mountain driftwood
littering the flash-fire chaparral.
Impassable interlocker. Towhee-coral.
Fertile ash.

If I were the designer,
I'd have drawn it taller, just enough
room for one beneath its kinked copper-wire
lightning rods,

and wider-leafed,
its lichen-green more suitably skewed
to intercept drifting rain so fine
it can be breathed.

But see
how it thrives in the oil-slick soils
and skidrock gullies flanking the canyon highways
above Half Moon Bay.

Minor, ornamental,
unfit for timbering, ideal
for aquaria, parrot perches, patio sculpture, barbecues.
We know its uses.

VIRGA

What goes up. What was broken.
What comes around. What lives.

What bears three leaves. What spared the rod.
What started out as just five loaves.

What's signified. What glisters.
What can look you in the eye.

What grows in where hair once was.
What saves the snows of yesteryear.

What turns plum-purple in the starlight.
What was denied against a knife-point.

What the sentences set loose.
What to strain for in the silence.

LINES FOR ROBINSON JEFFERS AT CARMEL POINT

> *Sleepe after toyle, port after stormie seas,*
> *Ease after warre, death after life does greatly please.*
> —Edmund Spenser, *The Faerie Queene*

Jeffers, you flinty sympathist of granite,
poet/homilist, provincial seer
and storm-bird, let it rest. Your work is finished.
They have no use for grand abstraction here.

Though Tor House tower is a faerie eyesore
marring the suburb's Hockneyesque regime,
all will fall. Despair is the worst evil.
You wrote it on the dark side of the beam.

Hendecasyllabics for Robert Frost

Truth? A pebble of quartz?
—Robert Frost, *For Once, Then, Something*

VISIONS. Seventeen-pick-up-truck collisions
shot in hi-def. A timely perfect circle
rainbow bangling the starboard wing. Each dusk brings
boozy seafog to numinize the driveway.
Gimmicks; tricks of the light. So it's no wonder
we (if ever we give our full attention)
stare the images into pixilation.

    Driving once through the desert past Loreto,
flame-tipped Palo Adán and white-faced ospreys
speed-blurred in the arroyos, I saw something
so unlikely I had to see it closer,
get it right to the light. It looked so strangely
miniature—like a petting zoo delinquent.
Weeks of summer had cured the flesh from maggots,
though, of course, it was dead: a bighorn yearling.
Someone (Who?) had arranged its hind- and forelegs
prancingly, so its jaunty hooves seemed almost
ice-fringed, cantering moonward off a rooftop…
Bungee cords double-looped around a signpost
strung it up like a totem. Teenage mischief?
Common cruelty? A sleeps-with-fishes message?
Someone killed it, or found it dead and lucky,
worth publicity. Anyone could see it.

Out-of-Work Song

Days away and there's little
to fiddle with. Nimblenessless
on the handle. I dangle
headlong in newfangleness
struggling to tug up my dress
so my don'ts won't show.
Words come slow, and vie
to be the best lie. Why I
ever tried to juggle
apples and metaphors
on this tight wire is
no idle quibble. I'm
trouble-tired. Double-
time rhymes go jingle
on a keyring to nothing.

Revisionary

for Kay Ryan

We sharpen our
lapidary eyes
toward flaws, and see
the easy cz disguise,
the phrase too pleased
to please. We loupe
the soldering for tell-tale
fracturing. We
will not be fooled.
But let us withdraw
the ball-peen hammer
from its velvet
swaddling, let us
address the listing
prong, the innocuous
ding: we stammer;
we miss the mark;
—with what great care
we over-swing.

III

What if I burst the fleshly Gate —
And pass Escaped — to thee!

—Emily Dickinson, #305

A Charm

I mumble through my words to find
a charm against her darker mind,
a garlic necklace, sheath of lead
as prophylactic to her dread.
Strip the heavens of the moon
to make my love a wrist-balloon.
Unscrew the daffodils; de-vein
the blood orange; winnow the grain
from the vodka; dehydrogenize
the Twinkie; blind the tuber's eyes;
teach the friarbird to pray;
lemon-juice the Milky Way.
Or, if she'll be better cheered,
cross wires with words and make them weird:
Pessary, Lorazepam,
Lunette, Samsara, Dithyramb,
Obeah, Pollard, Klaxon, Kohl,
Vibrissa, Bibelot, Girasol,
lend her your mystery, and bless
her luckless hours with puckishness.

Poems for Yosano Akiko

We fell in love in September.
Now the diesel gnarl of October, idling,
four years later.

~

4 a.m. Standing water
in the sink. Even the late-rising moon
has beaten me home.

~

Beware the scree path
to the clifftop, the shortcut
under One Fish Bay.

~

Though I love to walk
the sand the surf makes firm
I keep my cuffs dry.

~

The smell of hay
and orchard-sour
above the sound of waves.

~

An icicle forms
around what? Perilous firmness
of the unseen world.

~

Whatever stirs
beneath the beach rose thickets
doesn't ask me in.

Domestic

My lover can't get out of bed.
I carry in cold from the street.
I pile the new mail on the old
and make the canned vegetables neat.

And fix something good on the stove
to fill the whole house with a hunger.
And muffle the knife on the board.
And touch with the tips of my fingers.

And lock every window and door.
And throw all the windowshades open.
My lover can't make up her mind
whether today's meant to happen.

To lie down beside her might help
but I worry to make the suggestion—
an emptiness hangs from the hook
of even the gentlest question.

Beneath my uncertain caresses
her thoughts keep on turning to threat
as though I've been doing some violence
she can't confess to yet.

Sic

That thing you were about
to say—before my runaway
joke broke up the scene
bang-clang, dragging
spark-spray from the punchline—is gone
to the tip of someone else's tongue,
blister to an unknown burn.
What words I miss
every time I stop your mouth
with mine. There must be
a kennel where they sleep
till the owner's home, a run
of grass along the fence,
a never-ending bone. They're trained
which hand to lick, which door
to die for, who to sic.
Someday the porch light flicks on
they'll hear your whistle through the wall
and pull the kennel master
limb from limb.

Anonymous Brothel Photo, 1882

The only certain thing is that she's young.
Or is she? Pull away the veil of hair
blurring the edges of her eyes. Defer
for a moment the fringe of coverlet that hangs
self-consciously across her pelvic wings,
the strap a primper tugged down from her shoulder.
Try to return her uninflected stare
persuading you, *This is where I belong.*
There is no elsewhere. Paisley; worn divan;
hydrangeas; satin cushions in a row;
for backdrop, two black cloths that won't quite join:
eternal props of an artist's studio.
The boxing of her skin in stocking net—
skyscraper lights no one had dreamed of yet.

Anonymous Brothel Photo, 1885

Overexposure; light-wash. Even her fingers,
splayed in approximation of desire,
lose their singleness. Even the hair
that flares across her neck and shoulders singes
the too-receptive paper. The light changes
everything—her legs bent like a soldier
trampled in the field become tined spears
of lightning; a yoke of flame was once a string
of costume pearls. Who wouldn't wish to be
refined this way, blessing, blessed with light,
unreal to any vision but the mind's?
Then, sun might be a flicker of the sky
and not the flashpan's overbearing white,
the skin's cinched corset virtually unbound.

Insomnia

Even before I can fall asleep, I dream
alarm.

Yes, now I'm sure. This one is just like the one before
the one after.

O, for a new monotony!

Months ago you and I spoke, but we
never again.

I search for true constancy.
Let π be my example.

This is the round of eternity—
echoes, and the echoes they'll echo.

His Bed

after Robert Herrick's "Her Bed"

Picture a satin platter, serving up
the undigested remnants of a day,
the half-chewed fears, the fecalized desires
voided by viscid whiskey sleep. Picture
red emptiness, a hole with yellow hair.
This, love, is my bed, and I sleep there.

Heart Murmur

When it's not there, everything's normal. Days
        prowl or scamper, swim howl or play dead
        with an animal's pure regard for surfaces,
        no sense of absence, nothing underlying.
        A cut thumb merely bleeds and stings
        and a squirrel's pushpinned eye is a curious thing.

Then it comes, or I do, into the world where
        there is no being without it. A doubling
        murmur in the heart's chamber
        twins all things with their sordid nature.
        It rips you right in two. Careful, friend,
        which one of me it is you're comforting.

Poem with a Five O'clock Shadow

I hang up my good clothes, redeploy my books.
I Windex ants in the stickiness,
brandish a broom halfheartedly
at two pigeons cozying above the breezeway.

For the fruit flies I make no excuses.
Red-goggled copulating
opportunists crotch-sniffing beer bottles
and kiwi rinds, any stinking thing.

Then the hours come rabbling in
with their cigarette burns and their cups outstretched.
I do what I can. I please the first with cream,
but these five smirk at anything but gin.

Call me the bedwrecker, the ruthless
rainwatcher. Call me fat-lipped joy.
I put my lover on a plane this morning.
Separate. Still practicing.

Long-Distance Sonnet

Here, fat raindrops shatter. There, it's clear
and far too cold for rain. I try to imagine
Anywhere: a smoke-blind gare du nord
where stragglers climb into their red-eyed dream,
but I can't change our silhouette to theirs.
You walk back home from work, and the same keys
turn the same locks. The morning paper's thin.
You read it last week—you know what it says.
You and I want correspondences,
not eat-sleep repetition. Some routine
bloodletting of the cause beneath the is,
some wound for us to stick our fingers in
that heals, but seals us in its hidden scar,
so when at last the rain gives out, you're here.

Mirrorform

I don't disappear——
I keep this blank filled in——
I hold my end of the line——
You'll always find me here.

Hearts waver. Year on year
transfigures and decays
my stranded DNA.
I don't disappear.

From the Interim

The rain falls down and won't get up again.
Strangers fill the room,
begging my empty chairs away
then sitting down alone.
I'm waiting. This must be a waiting room.

The trains zoom out and in. They run on rain,
which translates into steam.
The rain-trains keep their secret regimen,
whisking the right CVs to the right addresses
for their gathering successes.

The last thing left to do is to begin.
I wait to wait to wait to wait again
listening
for updates from the interim between
goodbye and gone.

ACKNOWLEDGEMENTS

Thanks to the editors of the following journals and anthologies in which these poems first appeared, sometimes in slightly different versions or under different titles: *32 Poems*: "Invitation"; *Able Muse*: "Camerado"; *The Antioch Review*: "Lines for Robinson Jeffers at Carmel Point"; *Breakwater*: "Sic"; *Crazyhorse*: "Insomnia"; *Drunken Boat*: "Karsilama," "Long-Distance Sonnet"; *Fourteen Hills*: "First Fig," "Second Fig"; *Innisfree Poetry Journal*: "Poem with a Five O'clock Shadow"; *Linebreak*: "Triolet for a Bad Obsession"; *Lo-Ball*: "His Bed," "Swish"; *The Pennsylvania Review*: "Anonymous Brothel Photo, 1882"; *Ploughshares*: "Revisionary," "Universal Movers"; *Poet Lore*: "Poems for Yosano Akiko"; *Poetry Miscellany*: "Diurnal"; *Smartish Pace*: "Anonymous Brothel Photo, 1885"; *Southwest Review*: "A Charm"; *Southern Poetry Review*: "Overture," "Long Division"; *Subtropics*: "Heart Murmur," "From the Interim"; *Terrain.org*: "Manzanita"; *The The Poetry Blog*: "Love-Busker"; *Tin House*: "Minotaur"; *Your Impossible Voice*: "Deviants," "An Encounter"; *ZYZZYVA*: "On Seeing Fiona with Her New Lover".

I am grateful for the fellowship support I received while working on this collection from the Creative Writing Programs of Stanford University and the University of Virginia. I owe an enormous debt of gratitude to the teachers who guided me along the way, particularly to Eavan Boland, Steve Cushman, Simone Di Piero, Rita Dove, Deborah Eisenberg, Joseph Epstein, Ken Fields, Reg Gibbons, Mary Kinzie, Greg Orr, Lisa Russ Spaar, and Charles Wright. Thanks to Kimberly Verhines, Laura Davis, and everyone at SFA for believing in my work. Thanks also to David Lykes Keenan for the cover photograph, and to Alex Burke for the use of his image. This book could not have been completed without the invaluable assistance and critical input of Kim Addonizio, James Arthur, Jennifer Foerster, Keetje Kuipers, Randy Mann, Doug Powell, Matthew Siegel, Bruce Snider, and Greg Wrenn. My dear friends, you inspire me. To my parents, I owe more than I can possibly say. Thank you. And to Brittany Perham, my first reader—*As far as Cho-fu-Sa*, and farther.

About the Author

PETER KLINE teaches creative writing at the University of San Francisco and at Stanford University, where he was a Chace Lecturer. A former Wallace Stegner Fellow at Stanford, he is also the recipient of residency awards from the James Merrill House, the Amy Clampitt House, and the Kimmell Harding Nelson Foundation. His work has appeared in *Poetry, Ploughshares, Tin House,* the *Best New Poets* series, and elsewhere. A graduate of Northwestern University and the University of Virginia, he currently lives in San Francisco.

CPSIA information can be obtained at www.ICGtesting.com
Printed in the USA
BVOW04s1241161113

336310BV00004B/10/P